Walk Song

David Herd

Walk Song

Shearsman Books

First published in the United Kingdom in 2022 by
Shearsman Books
P O Box 4239
Swindon
SN3 9FN

Shearsman Books Ltd Registered Office
30–31 St. James Place, Mangotsfield, Bristol BS16 9JB
(this address not for correspondence)

www.shearsman.com

ISBN 978-1-84861-842-8

Contents

Prologue

This prologue is not a poem
It is an act of welcome
It announces
That people present
Reject the terms
Of a debate that criminalizes
Human movement
It is a declaration this night
In Shepherdswell
Of solidarity.

It says that we have started –
That we are starting out –
That by the oldest action
Which is listening to tales
That other people tell
Of others
Told by others
We set out to make a language
That opens politics
Establishes belonging
Where a person dwells.
Where they are now
Which is to say
Where we are now
Walking
In solidarity
Along an ancient track
That we come back to the geography of it
North of Dover
That where the language starts
Now longen folk to goon
On this pilgrimage.

In June not April
And with the sweet showers far behind us
Though with the birds singing
And people sleeping
With open eye
And what we long for
Is to hear each other's tales
And to tell them again
As told by some hath holpen
Walking
So priketh him nature
Not believing the stories
Our officials tell.
Because we know too much
About what goes unsaid
And what we choose to walk for
Is the possibility of trust
In language
To hear the unsaid spoken
And then repeated
Made
Unambiguous and loud
Set out over a landscape gathered
Step by step
As by virtue of walking which
We call our commons
Every sap vessel bathed in moisture
And what that commons calls for
Is what these stories sound.

Of crossing
For to seken straunge strondes

In moments of emergency
Whan that they were seeke
Of tribunals
Where the unsaid goes unspoken
Lines of questioning
No official has written down
People present by video
Answers mistranslated
As outside by the station
At the dead of morning
As the young sun rises
Woken in their homes
People are picked up and detained.
Routinely and
Arbitrarily
In every holt and heeth
Under the sun while
Smale foweles maken melodye
And why we walk is
To make a spectacle of welcome
This political carnival
Across the Weald of Kent
People circulating
Making music
Listening to stories
People urgently need said.

And said
And said again
Stories of the new geography
Stories of arrival
Of unaccompanied minors

Of people picked up and detained
Of process
And mistranslation
Networks of visitors and friends
This new language we ask for
Forming
Strung out
Along the North Downs Way.

Which makes it a question of scale.
Consider just
The scale
Of the undertaking
Chaucer's pilgrims crossing
Palatye and Turkye and Ruce
Across the Grete See
Which is the Mediterranean
Dark these days
Not like wine
Crossing through Flaundres
Through Artoys
Crossing the water at Pycardie.
And all the while finding stories
And then all of them
Gathering one night in London
And so the Host says
Since we're walking
Why don't we tell each other tales
And so they do
Out of Southwark
And what comes of Southwark
Is a whole new language

Of travel and assembly and curiosity
And welcome.

To make his English sweete.
That's why Chaucer told his tales.
How badly we need English
To be made sweet again
Rendered hostile by act of law
So that even friendship is barely possible –
There as this lord was kepere of the celle –
So we might actually talk
And in talking
Come to understand the journey –
Tender
Says the poet
To Canterbury they wende.

Tender
To hold
From the French
Tendre
From the English
For listening
To a story as it is said
To attend
Tendre
And then writing it down
Because it isn't written
Because the hearings
In the British immigration system
Are not courts
Of record.

So there are no stories
And people leave
As if there never had been
Stories
And so nobody
Who reaches a verdict
Has a real story
With which to contend
So now we are telling them
En masse
And people will listen
In sondry londes
And specially
From every shires ende.

But this prologue is not a poem
It is an act of introduction
Bathed every veyne in swich licour
And all the introduction can do
Is set the tone
Albeit the tone
Is everything
And the tone is welcoming
And the tone is celebratory
And the tone is courteous
And the tone is real
And every step sets out a demand
And every demand is urgent
And what we call for
Is an end
To this inhuman discourse.

And so we stop this night

And the Host steps up
And he says
Listen to this story
Whan that Aprille with his shoures soote
And the room goes quiet
And a voice starts up
And then the language
Alters
Sweet
Tender
Perced to the roote.

June 2015

I Recall It was Different

I recall it was different, yes,
And those days were more than brutal
The iron, I remember,
Went in deep
Fixed
Against the sun
And where we had imagined
The future
Eclipsed
Towards the land
This was the logic
We had become

Songs
from the Language
of a Declaration

1. Whereas

Whereas
Lilac
Bloomed
Against the billboards
Albeit torn
Besides the building
Where the sun
Broke in

And whereas people
And all the talk
And all the gatherings
Towards equality
And the rose
And the wood pigeon
Against an open field

And whereas
The distance
Which we would collapse
Into intimacy
Broken against the language
Of a difficult day

And whereas
The heart
Gave out
And whereas
We repudiated
The nation

And it was warm
And against the narrative
People articulated
Their way

And whereas
It was not so much
And since
Nobody thought
That it was sovereign
Like the wisteria didn't
Or the people
Since this was time
To walk

Start out
Against the ground
And whereas people
Being people
Where the goldfinch
Against the backdrop
Where the silence
Stalks

And whereas
The state
And whereas the mechanism
Was arbitrary
Where the heart
And where the lungs
And whereas the stamina
Gave way

Where people walked
Against that fact
And whereas the language
Relented
Briefly
Against the building
Where the lilac
Lay

Where the geography
Held good
Where it was that nobody
Reported
Where we sat
Unbeknownst to anybody
Against an open field
That day
You spoke
And whereas everything
In abeyance
State
Lilac
We heard the language
Yield

2. And in Accordance

And whereas
In accordance
With an actual narrative
Where the state
Against the backdrop
Of an open
Sky
Stopped
Against the ground
Where
In accordance
With the geography
Where the lilac
Against the sycamore
Where the dogwood
Lies

Where the language
Laid out
Where the argument
Was against
Departure
Formulated as a syntax
People were compelled
To leave
Held good
Against the ground
And whereas the context
Was briefly birdsong
Sweet

Against the violence
Where as the narrative needs

Whereas
A collective
Takes shape
And whereas nobody
Registered
It was happening
As deep they went
Into the morning
Like Scheherazade
Witness
To the fact
And everybody present
Was breathing
In solidarity
Or something
As the language
Heeds.

3. As Well as in Association

As well as
In association
And as well as
The better abstractions
We are capable of
The way between us
As we approached
The capital
We carried all
And each

The way the land
Dropped back
And as well as
The depth of conversation
Or say the extent
Or say the implication
We pictured a language
It was necessary
To reach

Or as well as
The field
As it opened out
And as much as
We were conscious
Sometimes
Of the ground beneath us
Not as category
But in our occupation

The way we watched the landscape
Turn
Quietly
As it dropped
Towards the coast
And what we came to articulate
Was a moment of delicacy
Of tact
Pictured as continuity
As a series of coordinates
It was possible to learn

The way that people carried
Without a map
That as well as in association
That as they gathered
Before the capital
Irrespective
Of the State

Lilac
Holding good
That whereas in recognition
Open
Against the language
It was determined
They would wait.

4. At the Time When

At the time when
It was committed
And the state knew
Impunity
Designated
Arbitrarily
Under the authority
Of the court

At that time
As it was meant
As the change was
Realized
Upon us
Legislated
Against the landscape
That time it was broken
As people thought

Even as the colours
Held good
And the seasons stretched out
Regular
Towards us
So this was summer
And still it was possible
Our democracy
Could fall
Hard
Against the grass

As it was recognized
The change
Was upon us
Bloodless
Against the lilacs
Even as the language
Formed

Even as we drove
Ourselves
Across the state
Witness
To a million
Particulars
The day the wind dropped
And as though we were waiting
The geese came through
Called
Against the light
At that time when the brushings
Were upon us
Beside the graves
Against the mountains
It was violence
That people knew

As if it was that they were witness
To that fact
And as if it was possible
To lift
From history
Stutter

Into the discourse
Against the authority
Of the court

That time it dawned
The change
Was suddenly
Upon us
Startled
Into language
People
Fought

5. As a Last Resort

As a last
Resort
We might contemplate
The bodies

Lined up
By way of argument
In some kind of
Ordinary street

Pushed back
Towards the glass
And whereas the discourse
Alters

Against the ground
Towards the language
This is violence
People meet.

Given
As historical fact
As the language practises its slow
Violence

Audible
Against the landscape
As the bodies in outline
Against the grass

Lilac
Held in hand
Since this is not
Prophecy

Only history
Shaped like syntax
People witnessing
Push back.

6. Whether Alone or in Community

This song is to anybody
Whether alone
Or in community
Those keeping
Or in observance
Those who
Shall be held

It is from the trees
Who listen out
To those as well
In association
From the ground
As the season falters
In recognition everywhere
As call to change

Anybody
Who seeks
Against perhaps the backdrop
Of the mountains
Set forth solely
For the purpose
Susceptible
To any act

Who would be held
As once they had
Whether political
Or jurisdictional

At the time even
When it was committed
At its dissolution
Turned back.

To anybody who stands
Or who had imagined
Standing
Watching the roof smoke
Against the perimeter
Witnessing the constitution
Fall

Who knows
At dead of night
That this is actually
The circumstance
Within the burden
Of each state
Who is denied
The law

Who would act
Or would be held
Anybody shall be subjected
In the quiet
Before it was applicable
Who stood listening to the birds
Or pictured that he might
Imagining
A full equality
As he carried that acoustic

Waiting as the language
Turned

To anybody
Who sleeps
Whether alone
Or with belongings
Who occupies
The background
As the earth
Curves

Who stands
This dead of night
Whether left
Or in association
At that time
When it is committed
Who would walk
Towards

7. And at its Dissolution

And at its dissolution
I think that day the trees were visible
As you were surely
Beside the billboard
Against all the instruments
Of the State
Laid down
Against the grass
And clear as it was to anybody
What had to be defended
As you breathed surely
Besides the lilac
That was the next day
They did not pass.

Even as they came
And as that time the emotion was political
At its dissolution
When the trees were visible
And I think you laid
The bird song
Bare
Not speaking
As if it was the past
But plainly as the discourse
Surrounds us
As you spoke and as
I think we gathered
Then that day also
They did not pass.

And at that time we listened
With nothing left
And what we heard you issue
Was a declaration
At its dissolution
When the State was visible
And as we heard you breathe
You brought the language
Back
Articulated
The way it broke
Taught us how to name
The violence
As it gathered
With you among us
As we stood
They did not pass.

8. In a Full Equality

To anybody who would imagine
A full equality
Who would listen
Against the backdrop
As the earth
Turns
Softly
At dead of night
Would sing the outline
Of an algorithm
Would gesture
Towards their lover
Would know at least their lover
Yearns

If not exactly
For the same
Who would stand there as the crowd
Assembles
As the boat rocks
Against the distance
And whereas the State
Turns back
Would be held
As once they had
Or at least as they imagined holding
In the half light of the polity
Before they heard
The polity
Collapse

Or at least as they imagined that it might
Who would know perhaps
A series of belongings
Picked out
Against the morning
They had been prepared
To leave
Witness
Against that fact
Would carry back
A sprig
Of lilac
Against the darkness
Of an interruption
Who listened while their lover
Breathed

Or breathes
Who breathes
Anybody would imagine
Sleeping
Who was watched over
Or perhaps was watching
As a person slept
Their last
Who was carried
Before that fact
And who might make their love song
A proposition
Who was lifted
Perhaps in isolation
Who remembered they had the stamina
To act

Who speaks
Or who would start
Anybody imagined speaking
Or perhaps had found themselves
Against the outline
Of a person's
Voice

Who had listened
Towards that sound
And when that day the people
Assembled
When the line formed
Out of intimacy
Who made
Some noise

9. With Others and In Public

We are echoed everywhere
Pictured as a full equality
Whether with others
Or perhaps in public
Or whether it was a morning
In which anybody
Might take part
Figured
Like the build up of a day
In which perhaps our talking
Was one of our actions
I think maybe about the weather
Or a best friend's passing
How even the way he stumbled
Became the grand collage

Like he wanted to add something
To what we had
Or whereas even to contemplate
That prospect
Like that billboard you sent me
Washed up against a building
Documenting the items
Of a person's rights
That anybody
Might add
Or that we might depict a language
As we walked
Following the morning
Added to that detail
In a common light

10. And Now Therefore

And now therefore
This morning
We are at the season's edge
Where the swallows
And the house martins
Prepare to leave us
Turned
Towards the sun
And whereas the tree line
Waits
Burnt
In its image
We count the day's
Elements

Corn
For a friend
Because it shoulders
Our belonging
And where the ground has hardened
We count the morning's dew
For another
Who walked
One who witnessed rivers
And mountains
Turned back
Towards the water
As it were compelled
To choose

At the edge
This morning
Where the season dries
And alters
And the birds know
That a winter
Is coming in
And we know
As we watch
These are the days
Define us
Sky
Reached out
Therefore now
And

August 2019

Letter to a Friend

Dear Anupama
And now again I am in Trivandrum
Called towards your city against a southern sky
By your metaphors of trust and your patiently
Unfolded syntax as we sit
Speaking towards the ocean
Folded through your summer
Against the decade's lies.
Spoken in each place.
As we decide to walk like strangers
Where the traffic echoes against the buildings
And we find language through the trees
As if that welcome we spoke of
Was simply the street
And what we catch are the intimacies
Of traders
Through the dust
I picked up on my boot soles
Carried across a city
I couldn't bring myself to leave.
And which your letter unfolded
Takes me back
Anupama I am in Trivandrum
And it is late and the city is talking
And I follow the syntax
Of the streets
Tired but alive
Through all the consonants of Malayalam
Naming flowers
Cradled against the mountains
Listening for those secrets
To which your language leads.

As if we might be named
Simply by what we see
Perhaps in all its beautiful inflorescence
As Krishna Kireedam
Or Araali
The flower they called the South Sea Rose
As from your balcony
At night
We traded poetry
For politics
Like people
Woven through a city
Following the syntax
Home.

Still Spring

January

I

These trees are backlit
Angled to the east
On this first morning
The year seems bright

As we gather
Promising
No grounds for optimism
Seagulls lifting
First light

II

Notwithstanding the rain
The trees sway gently
Dark against the backdrop
So I couldn't see the leaves
If there were any
Bark
Silver
Against the streetlights
Crosswires obsolete
No birds

III
On the question of scale
I think perhaps the trees will save us
Where we are intimate
Who listen
And this is the language of the birds

In its call
And its response
Who thought about a different learning
January
We argue
This is not gone

IV
I want to call this day
A place of refuge
In its openness
This morning
Articulated
By the light

Where the trees
And the birds
Come back again
Perceptibly
Soft
Into my headphones
You say it might

February

V
I think the thread
Denotes
Precarity
That song
I heard you singing
That I worried
Might break

Always
Each day
Your singularity
Stops me
Broke
I listened
Silence
Stayed

VI
You broke off
I mean
We were still talking
In my head
We had been abandoned
This was upper
New York State

And you
When you filed
You who braided

Everything
As the trees
Fell silent
We came into the morning
Late

VII
When I put my arms around you
I can feel your body weight
I know, in your heaviness,
You have travelled this far

I can see it in your eyes
You have been
Overwhelmingly rejected
You ask
After my children
Still
You care

VIII
I come back not
To the political geography
Figured
Into the skyline
Where the light
Goes grey

People
Holding out
I come back to trees

And fragments
Where the boat rocks
In the morning
I catch you
Dazed

IX
I come back to the trees
Shrouded in mist today
The morning is the emergence
Of a dispersed light

No thread
Across the sky
None of that
Violent certainty
Beauty
Where the night stops
We watch
Wait

X
Today perhaps these trees
Are not precarious
In their qualities
Established
By this February
Light
Not harsh today
You could think

These days were not
Ravaged
Brutalised
Where the logic
And the language
Bites

Deep
Into the skin
You could think the air was resting
And if you were
Hopeful
Some kind of life together
Qualified
By the sun
Against these trees
This morning in spring-like
February
Pictured
Against the backdrop
We set about imagining
Undone

March

XI
A bee floats by
I don't know what it is in search of
It looks heavy to me
Effortful
Draws my attention from the trees

Situated
Off grid
We start with a series
Of fragments
Which you piece
Some of them together
As if in solidarity
You breathe

XII
I catch you breathless
The world is with us
In your lungs
You draw deeply
From within its rhythms
And sometimes when you speak
It hurts

Fighting
To catch your breath
And I say
I am saying to you

What I can
Like that bee came
And you are breathing
And this is early
March

    XIII
I wanted the world
To be a different medium
When we spoke
I think you called it
Our transitional sense
Like light through glass
Language as disposed
To movement
You breathed
We watched the complications
Pass

Slowly
Into the world
Like we settled on a preposition
As though we were governed
Only towards your breathing
And as you walked
I watched you through
Easier in your step
Like somehow the medium
Had lightened
No questions today
Answered

Only maybe Spring
Or so

    XIV
I offer you
These early spring days
Since you were up late
Worrying
The future
Coming in
Hard
Into your breath
I listen as your wakefulness
Accumulates
Like capital
I give you apple blossom
You tell me what the night sweats
Bring

In the quietness
Of the night
I give you that sweet
Magnolia
Which we both know
In the morning
Will be short lived
Days
Before it drops
I give you the season's
Syllables
Yours

Against the future
No longer mine
To give

    XV
This plain light
Is what I have to offer you
This morning
I want to say milky
As it were
Becoming blue
Not milky
White
Plain against the ladder opposite
You were wakeful
You bring me the night's news

As it were
The cumulative effect
I sketch in the day's
Conditions
What I have to offer
Where you show me capital
Is the morning's light
That ladder they didn't use
And all those qualities
Obsolete
Spring
Into the trees now
In plain
Sight

XVI

Spring doesn't wait
And so we are collecting
Elements
Wrapped loose
Against the morning
And what the airs
Bring
As warmth
Calling people back
We count the absences
Of winter
Who registered
In passing
What the change
Leaves

That people started naming
Simply as such
Like in one of those
Epic
Roll calls
Issued quietly
As if in lyric
And what we had to speak about
Went unsaid
That magnolia
Passed
And where we walked the ground
Warming
Those trees
Lined up against the distance

Still
Out

   XVII
There are days
At this time of year
I mean almost exactly
This time of year
When the balance
Of elements
Is quite precise
When the sun
Hangs low
And we are almost
Blinded
Air
Unfathomable
Ground
Ice

When we know
We might tip back
This is almost winter
A man waves to me
While walking
He is not one of the dead
By the road
To
The contagious hospital
Sun rises
Least
Said

April

XVIII
April today and I think perhaps
The walk carries us
As the trees stand
No longer leafless
And the season enters
In the global north
Spring we had imagined
Or so
Pictured
Like a series
Of mechanisms
First the roots
Gripped intricately against
The darkness
Deep into the subsoil
Then the warmth

That each of us
Had come to know
As if the environment had become
Our decision
Since this was April
And the ground was open
By the road
Towards the rain
Heavy enough
Almost
To drown things out
Like the constant reminder

Of bird song
On main street
Where we saw people passing
In quiet acknowledgement
Of a person's pain

As if in fact they were people
We had come to know
Persons among us
We had gripped
Tightly
By whom we had been held
Or sometimes we had listened
Hardly anybody conscious
Of another's breath
Or another
Only the birds
Since this is April today
On Main Street
Paused almost
Momentarily
Then still
We walked

April 2020

Where We Harboured

Where we harboured
We had travelled far
From the trade winds
Drawn towards the safety
Of a small cove
Where we could stay
Maybe learn to fish
And we would dive from the edge
Like dolphins
And we would surface
Almost imagining
We could swim
Like whales

With the water against our face
Breaking back into the air above us
Gasping
And laughing
As the echoes came
Turned
Onto our backs
So we might be imagined
Floating
Captured
In the sunlight
Somewhere
Safe

Walk Song

1.
And therefore as fact
After the wind dropped
People gathered
Say that they assembled
As a body of persons
Say perhaps that they were intimate
Against the land
Pictured
The way it lay
Walked through and drawn
As context
After the context
Laid out against the language
Left no option
People came.

Let's call it walking
Towards the sun
With the sun and
Against the sun
Establishing a rhythm
As part of the process
In which the language
Might be thought to fold back
So that in talking
The terms return
And come back therefore
To the geography
The geography
To include Dartford
The geography to include

Gravesend
To include people
Occupying ground
Laid out and present
As particulars
Named perhaps
As part of the process
In which the magpie
Chatters back
As a kind of resolution
Observed as sound
Extrapolated out
In the name of politics
Carried
As people walk
Laid out against the sun
Across an ancient track.

As perhaps the morning sets out
And the question therefore forms
In walking
Since this is a dynamic
As the river widens
People watching the post-industrial
Fall into view
Articulating
The way things go
Held out against the old dichotomy
Of sky set out against water
Establishing the landscape
As the ground curves back
As a kind of setting

Where people start
Or given perhaps as the basis
Of an understanding
Taken
Under advisement
That walking is the last act.
Or if not final maybe
Taken back
The way a person
Registers experience
Witness perhaps
As part of the process
And then periodically
Taking stock
As the narrative
Draws back ground
And each time it is told
The geography alters
Adjusted again
Towards the horizon
As if in walking
He might not stop.

As if the way that people came
Or the way perhaps they
Carried
Their belongings
As the day lengthened
Towards a geography
No longer conceivable as map
Just people
Against the ground

Establishing terms
Against the discourse
Watchful
Where the bodies
Against the language
Drop.

2.
Let me clarify
This is a local action
Like the morning
In which the bird song
Illuminates
The sky
Situated
Against the light
And setting out
A whole arrangement
Of people
Registered present
Establishing a discourse
The way the landscape lies.

To constellate the terms
I mean that people
Constitute
The terms
Since it is plain
In the present moment
That to walk
Is to act
Unfold
What people know
Strung out clear
Across the new geography
Witness against the border
Drawing the language
Back
To a bearing

We might sustain
Written into the principle
Of movement
I name Rashid in this context
I name Kam
Visibly eloquent
Against the light
And for all the world
Walking
Plainly
By way of evidence
Carrying the argument
With them.

That a), people walk
Which is how the emphasis falls
In demonstration
Each step
A kind of guidance
So that the language
Might know the way
Not as discourse exactly
Just as fact
As a person steps up
Before the world
But b), that standing
Was suddenly subject
To recognition.
So that a person
Rendered vulnerable
Say for instance walking across a field
Or in a city

Conscious exclusively
That the narrative had changed
Darkened
Out of sight
Picking up just
Minimal possessions
Visible
In outline
Standing where the discourse
Ends
Pictured
At the edge
Stationed
Where we calculate
Belonging
So that we woke one morning
Against the tree line
Only to find our horizon
Had been reset
The whole argument
Laid out as space
And persons figured
In isolation
Stipulated
Outside the language.
It was for this
That people walked.

That they gathered
And then
We slept
And the way the morning

Becomes an intention
Startled
Against the horizon
People followed each other
Across the plain
Outwith
Not so much
Think of it like
Gathering to dance
Movement
Following movement
Different
Same.

3.
It comes back to an assertion:
That a person present
Carries an entitlement
Before the law
Laid down
Against the ground
Breathing openly
And softly
Sleeping
Among persons
Till the morning
Sounds.

Witness
The walk
Laid out evenly
Against the landscape
Articulated
Like a syntax
That would begin to form
Trees
Lined up against the light
People openly
And softly
Poised
Like a proposition
Undeniable
Before the law.
Rendered present
Simply as fact
Like saying

"These trees are amazing"
Linked intricately
Against an environment
Laid out equally
Against the light
Which walking
I think maybe we understand
This person brave
And surely beautiful
Conditioned
By the earth's dependency
Bearing geography
As political fact.

I think we recognize
This fact.
Maybe the way
A landscape
Registers its impression.
The way a person
Resting intermittently
Breathes heavily
Against the ground
Intimately even
As we start out
Leaving only the trees
Behind us
Exemplary of nothing
Only the way
A context sounds.
That people
Piece into place

Figure out
A network of prepositions
That one day
Somebody
Might stand before the law
In the entirety of what he knows
Call it
Degree zero
Testify
Uninterrupted
To the magnitude of his condition.

Towards which we angle against the land.
Standing by the coast in its impossible delicacy.
Witnessing
As water and sand
Give way
The ground
On which we sleep
People dreaming again
Towards tomorrow
All those
Complicated possibilities
That only people
Keep.

4.

Which is where perhaps
As such
With people recognized
As such
In the oldest action
Which we might call walking
People in solidarity
Along an ancient track
Structured
By the act
Which as the frequency levelled
We knew as listening
The language
As it is spoken
Called back.

I say it quietly
Knowing that only you
Will listen
Inward with the process
Surely for long enough
Intimate with the grounds
That only a complex
Of qualities
Susceptible always to alteration
Approximates a person
As such.
Like love
Which varies
Both in its degree
As in its intensity

I call on Seth
In his magnificent eloquence
To teach us about love
Patience
Folded through a life
Articulated plainly and with dignity
Broken sometimes
Against the language
Even as it is uttered
Called back.

So that to walk
With stories
Is to come back to the geography
The ground
A person rests on
Arched backwards towards the sky
Co-ordinated
Not by love
But by memories of necessity
Communicated against the language
The way the landscape lies
With people situated
As such
And therefore qualified
As such
Intimating
As part of the process
A context equal to the scale
Or say the depth
Or say the extent
Or say just the physical intensity

Of a geography underwritten
By a person's claim.

Pictured as a curve back towards to the sun.
And pictured as people walking
Towards the sun.
Grounded
In their solidarity
By an ancient track
As the terms are underscored
Written down as stones thereby
And rocks
People
Moving forwards
Carrying the language
Back.

5.
But this is not a proposition
The rocks seal
Nothing
However sweetly
In the sunshine
A person leans back
From the Latin
To persuade
As in *soote*
Svadu
Echoed sweetly
Against the language
The walk
Is an act.

Physically disposed
Since what we have here is
Figures in a Landscape
Occupied as part of the process not
With where the franchise stops
Just following a line
Which in its disposition today
Constitutes an argument
Visible from the city
Dropping from the ridge
As it approaches the coast.
Capable of myth
But this is not mythography
No predecession
Completing a sequence
Situating a person

Where they come to stand
Just bearings
In the middle of an act
Taken with the person
You happened to stand next to
Picturing
The possibilities
Plainly visible in relation to the land.
And therefore figured
In relation to a walk
And therefore figuring the landscape
In relation to a walk
Which is to say a person
Rendered present among persons
Figuring their relation
As a collective act
As in a frequency
Folded out toward the sound
In all its complexity
Unmistakable as bird song
People
Set out openly against the discourse
Picturing a language
Rendered capable of tact.

And sometimes equally laid out.
And not in any particular sequence.
Intervening
As part of the process
Each one following
As the names come through
Some voice

Calling people back
Bearing almost exactly perhaps
The emphasis necessary
Sweetly
With respect
What is it
That you do

June 2019

Acknowledgements

Some of these poems, sometimes in different versions, first appeared in *Refugee Tales III & IV, Harvard Review, This Corner, Almost Island* and *8 Arkusz*. 'Songs from the Language of a Declaration' was first published as a chapbook by Periplum, 'Walk Song' as a chapbook by Equipage, and 'Still Spring' as a pamphlet by Muscaliet Press. 'Prologue' was first published in *Refugee Tales I*. My warmest thanks go to the editors and publishers of these magazines and imprints: Anna Pincus, Ra Page, Neel Mukherjee, John Kinsella, Sharmistha Mohanty, Marta Koronkiewicz, Paweł Kaczmarski, Anthony Caleshu, Rod Mengham, Simon Eliot and Moyra Tourlamain. I am deeply grateful to Nancy Gaffield, Peter Gizzi and Denise Riley for their responses to individual sequences and poems, and to Steve Collis for being there every step of the way. Love and thanks go to everybody involved with the *Refugee Tales* project. This book is dedicated to Abi Cooper.

The Author

David Herd's collections of poetry include *All Just, Outwith*, and *Through*. He is Professor of Modern Literature at the University of Kent and co-organiser of the project *Refugee Tales*.